All inquiries should be addressed to:
Barron's Educational Series, Inc.
250 Wireless Boulevard
Hauppauge, NY 11788
http://www.barronseduc.com

Library of Congress Catalog Card No. 2001093216

ISBN-13: 978-0-7641-2118-0

Date of Manufacture : November 2014
Manufactured by : Shenzhen Wing King Tong Paper Products co.Ltd.,
Shenzhen, Guangdong, China

Printed in China

19 18 17

Don't Call Me Special

A FIRST LOOK AT DISABILITY

PAT THOMAS
ILLUSTRATED BY LESLEY HARKER

BARRON'S

Some children find it really hard to join in with sports and games in the playground.

How can you tell which ones?

You probably picked out the girl in the wheelchair.
Lots of people would guess that because
she has a disability she wouldn't be
interested in sports.

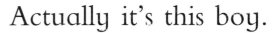

Actually it's this boy.

He hates sports because he can't run as fast as his friends and he always gets pushed around.

Sometimes when we see people who are different from us we assume things about them that are not always true.

When you assume, you are just making a guess. Assuming things about people can hurt their feelings and make them feel very left out.

Everybody in the world is unique. That means that each one of us is a little different from everyone else.

We each have things that we can do easily and things that we find hard and need help with.

What about you?

Do you know any children with a disability in your school? In your family?
What things are they good at? What do they find difficult?
What are you good at? What do you find difficult?

If you need glasses to see or special scissors to cut with, you are using special equipment to help you do your best.

What about you?

What kinds of disabilities do you know about? Can you think of some types of equipment (like glasses to help a person see) that help people with disabilities.

Children with disabilities often use helpful equipment, too. They use ramps to make getting from one place to another easier. They have special toilets and sinks or special types of mice and keyboards to help them use the computer.

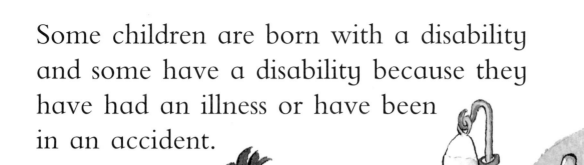

Some children are born with a disability and some have a disability because they have had an illness or have been in an accident.

There are many different types of disabilities. There are some where parts of your body don't work so well.

There are some that make it hard to learn as fast as others.

Years ago children with disabilities went to special schools with special teachers. Because of this people started calling them "special."

Today many people with disabilities dislike being called special because it makes them sound too different from everyone else.

Now many children with disabilities go to ordinary schools. That's because we know that the world is more interesting when we can all be together and learn from each other.

And even though children with disabilities may sometimes look different on the outside, inside they are just like you.

They feel angry and sad when they are teased and they feel happy and confident when they are accepted.

Some children with disabilities have extra teachers or helpers who work with them at school and at home. Sometimes these helpers are adults and sometimes they are children in the class.

A helper's job is just to help.
It can be very upsetting
when a helper tries to
do everything.

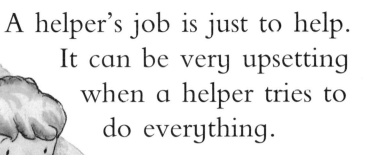

No two people learn things in the
same way or at the same speed.

Some children who have a disability
take longer to do or learn things,
or they do them in a
different way.

But sometimes they
can do things better
and learn things faster
than others.

We all need to work
and play together.

And with a little extra help, children with disabilities can learn and grow and do the things they want to – just like everybody else.

HOW TO USE THIS BOOK

This book is an introduction to the subject of disability for young children. The information a child needs to know, or can absorb, about disability varies from child to child and sometimes depends on the age of the child. In this age group it is important to foster acceptance and tolerance of people who are in some way "different." The whys about disability may be more appropriately addressed in detail with older children.

Sometimes adults need to sort out their own feelings about disability before talking to their children about it. It is only in recent years that we have begun to accept that disability does not need to be kept behind closed doors. Take some time to think through the issues before you talk to your child.

Group discussions about disability with young children can be very lively. One way to help children understand what it is like to have a disability is through play acting. A parent or teacher could help a child understand what it is like to be without one of their senses, for instance, by blindfolding them or putting headsets on their ears. In schools where equipment is available, giving able-bodied children the opportunity to use a wheelchair or other aids may enhance their understanding of some of the difficulties faced by someone who uses these aids.

After making it more difficult for children to see, hear, or walk, talk with them about people who have overcome disability, and even achieved greatness – such as Helen Keller, Beethoven, and Franklin Roosevelt.

Schools that are attended by a diversity of children must devise a variety of ways to help those less able. These may include ramps for wheelchairs, different scissors, paper, and pencils, adapted keyboards for computers (as well as different types of mice) and special tables and chairs. Discussions aimed at demystifying this equipment are important because they help us see the person and not the disability. They also foster creative problem solving. Get your child to talk about the different equipment people with disabilities use, perhaps as part of a wider discussion about the equipment others use to help them – a special stool in the bathroom, for example.

The language we use with regard to people with disabilities has come a long way, but many children with disabilities still get labeled, called names, and teased. Help your child to understand that name-calling (e.g., "cripple," "idiot," or "retard") is never acceptable. Likewise, help your child to use the right words to describe particular disabilities; words like "handicapped," "retarded," or "spastic" are now seen as hurtful and insulting.

Giving children responsibilities is a good way for them to learn. If there is a child with a disability in the class, make sure able-bodied students have a chance to be helpers.

Disability organizations, families, and self-help groups are often willing to come and talk to classes. These sessions can be very useful. A talk on sign language or lip reading, for instance, can widen children's horizons about listening and communication.

GLOSSARY

Assume When we assume something, we are making a guess without really knowing anything.

Equipment The things that we use to make some of the jobs we have to do easier.

Unique If something is unique, it is the only one of its kind. All people are unique because we are all different from each other. The things that make us unique make us special.

RECOMMENDED READING

Let's Talk About Needing Extra Help at School
by Susan Kent (PowerKids Press, 1999)

Talking About Disability
by Jillian Powell (Raintree Steck-Vaughn, 1999)

Just Kids: Visiting a Class for Children with Special Needs
by Ellen Senici (Dutton, 1998)

People with Disabilities
by Pete Sanders and Steve Myers (Copper Beach Books, 1998)

Author: A True Story
by Helen Lester (Houghton Mifflin, 1997)

Joey and Sam
by Illana Katz and Edward M. D. Ritvo (Real-Life Story Books, 1993)

CONTACTS

National Information Center for Children and Youth with Disabilities (NICHCY)
P.O. Box 1492
Washington, DC 20013-1492
(800) 695-0285; *www.NICHCY.org*

Family Resource Center on Disabilities
Room 300
20 East Jackson Boulevard
Chicago, IL 60604
(800) 952-4199

The Association for Persons with Severe Handicaps (TASH)
29 W. Susquehanna Avenue, Suite 210
Baltimore, MD 21204
(410) 828-8274

Roeher Institute
Kinsmen Building, York University
4700 Keele Street
North York, Ontario
M3J 1P3 Canada
(416) 661-9611; *info@roeher.ca*

The Arc of the United States
1010 Wayne Avenue, Suite 650
Silver Spring, MD 20910
(800) 433-5255; *Info@thearc.org*

American Academy of Pediatrics
141 Northwest Point Road
Elk Grove Village, IL 60009-0927
(800) 433-9016; *http://www.aap.org*